California Coastal Critters
A to Z

by

Shirley M. Price   **Merle E. Price**

Central Coast Press
San Luis Obispo, California 93403

CENTRAL COAST PRESS
P. O. Box 3654
San Luis Obispo, California 93403

ISBN: 978-1-930401-9-45

Technical support: Krzysztof Garlej

All photo images by Shirley M. Price and Merle E. Price except photo of condors courtesy of Arlene Fink and photos of breaching bottlenose dolphin and breaching humpback whale courtesy of Kera Mathes.

Front cover: View from the authors' family ranch on the Central Coast
Frontispiece: Central California coastline with authors' family ranch in distance

The California coastline extends for over a thousand miles along the Pacific shore from the redwood forests in northern California to the wide sandy beaches in the south. The natural beauty of this coast is known throughout the world.

It is the Central Coast, however, where the rugged Santa Lucia Mountains abruptly meet the sea that holds a special place in our hearts. For it is here, just south of the Monterey County line at the southern most end of Big Sur, that the Price family ranch that has been home to our family for over a century is located.

While large portions of the state and sections of the coast have been developed and urbanized, because of its remoteness and inaccessibility, this stretch of the coast remained relatively untouched through time. However, since completion of construction of California Highway One in 1937 which provided access to this region, more and more visitors have come to see this previously isolated area. Today, during the summer months and school breaks, a constant stream of cars make their way up and down the narrow, cliff hugging coastal highway, a highway considered by many as one of the most scenic in the world.

More than its scenic beauty, however, what makes this region truly magical, and what may not be immediately apparent to visitors, is the amazing diversity of native wildlife that call the California Central Coast home. Coastal California provides the ideal environment for land and marine mammals, fish and other marine life, birds, reptiles, amphibians, and insects of all kinds to thrive, both permanent residents and migrating species.

For us, it is extraordinary to be able to sit in front of our small ranch house or to peer out the window and see deer grazing in the meadow, or a coyote leaping about the pasture as it pursues some small quarry, or a bobcat slinking in the tall grass, or a hawk or turkey vulture circling above, or even a migrating whale spouting close to shore.

We began photographing the animals on the ranch and gradually the idea for this book, California Coastal Critters A to Z, came about. As we got more and more into the project, it became a wonderful excuse to research and visit wildlife viewing areas up and down the coast, camera in hand, to find and photograph coastal wildlife. Merle, who grew up on the Central Coast and was well coached by his father, Enos Price, seems to have an instinctive sense about the various animals' whereabouts and habits, such as which ones are out and about in the early morning, which ones appear at dusk, which are nocturnal, which are year round residents and which ones migrate to the coast to spend the winter. He's the "spotter," somehow always the one to spot an animal track, the movement of a small branch, a flutter of wings or the telltale call of a nearby bird. Shirley would follow behind, juggling the camera and lenses, trying to snap the perfect picture.

It has taken us two years or more to find and photograph the critters in the book, which, of course, is nowhere near a comprehensive guide to all the species of wildlife one might encounter on the coast. We've learned in the process that in addition to a good camera and proper light, a great deal of patience and luck is required. Rising at sunrise and sneaking out into the brush morning after morning or staying up way past bed time, both of which we've done, was no guarantee that we would spy let alone capture a great photo of some elusive critter. As we never seemed able to photograph a breaching whale or dolphin, Kera Mathes, a marine biologist and photographer, generously allowed us to include photos from her wonderful collection. A friend and neighbor, Arlene Fink, graciously provided the photo of the pair of endangered condors on the coast in Big Sur. Since we encountered a number of striking domestic animals residing on the coast while working on the project, we have included some of these.

Under the best of conditions, life for the native wildlife is difficult. They must hunt for food almost every waking hour while being on guard to avoid becoming someone else's meal at that time or any other. Sadly, some animals that were commonly found near the home place during Merle's childhood or previous times are now endangered or threatened. With the increasing human population, the effects of climate change, and the loss and degradation of natural habitats due to urban sprawl and development, polluted runoff, water diversions and the like, their survival will likely become more difficult.

Fortunately, federal, California state and local government agencies, private foundations and corporations such as the Hearst Corporation, as well as grass root citizen groups and concerned individuals, have taken and are taking steps to address the conservation needs of the Central Coast and the California coast as a whole. But the future continued success of these efforts and the long-term survival of the rich biodiversity for which coastal California is known depends upon educating residents and visitors, especially the young, about our native wildlife, plants and habitats and the crucial need to protect and preserve them. This book barely scratches the surface, but we hope it will inspire readers to learn more about coastal wildlife species and habitats, thereby increasing their respect and appreciation of them and ultimately to support efforts to protect and preserve these national treasures for future generations to come.

A

is for

abalone

Once commonly found clinging to rocks on the Central Coast shore,
This true California native is rarely found anymore.

anemone

This tide pool creature's flower-like tentacles gently sway
Until touched, and their sharp sting snares some passing prey.

angus

These hornless cattle with a solid black coat of hair
Can be found grazing on Central Coast ranches everywhere.

B

is for

barn swallow

A spot under the eaves was deemed the safest and best
By a pair of swallows building their mud and grass nest.

bluebird

With his keen eyes peeled, the bluebird on his perch will stay,
Then spotting an insect, will swoop down to seize his prey.

bobcat

Named for its short bobbed tail, this cat with the spotted fur
May be observed hunting on the coast near Big Sur.

C

is for

condor

This pair of endangered condors are zoo-reared birds
Released in Big Sur where they're closely monitored.

cormorant

On offshore rocks colonies of these large black seabirds thrive,
Dining on fish they catch below the surface when they dive.

coyote

This wily hunter tracks a scent and keeps his sharp eyes peeled to capture a tasty morsel in the grassy field.

crow

This clever black bird who can be a noisy pest
Would score very high on an intelligence test.

crab

Tide pools on the rocky Pacific seashore
Are home to crabs and other marine life galore.

D

is for

deer

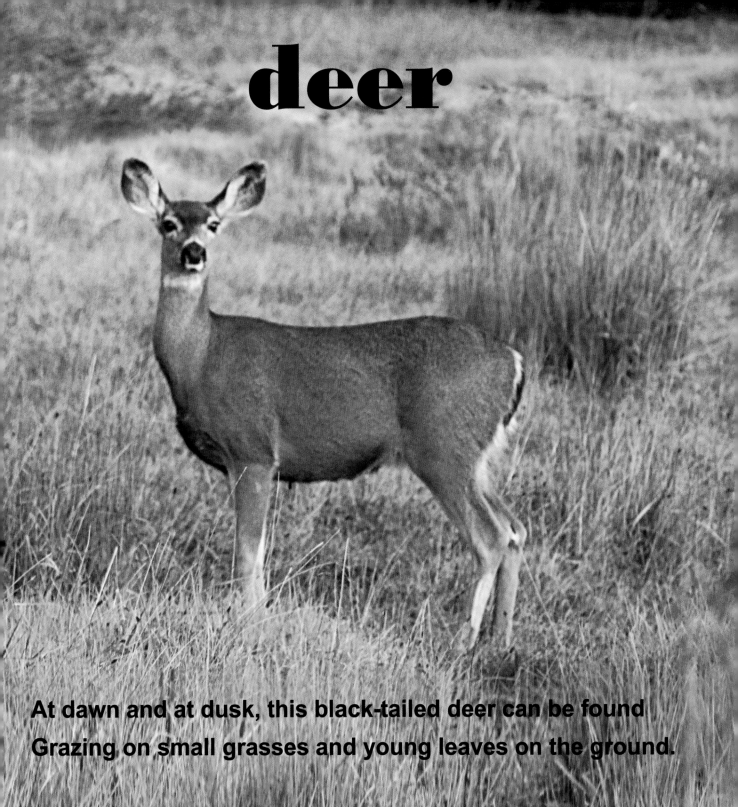

At dawn and at dusk, this black-tailed deer can be found
Grazing on small grasses and young leaves on the ground.

dolphin

Playful dolphins offshore can put on quite a show,
Breaching, somersaulting and diving below.

donkey

"EEE AWE, EEE AWE" the gentle pet with the big ears brayed,
Charming those within earshot with his donkey serenade.

duck

The shiny green-headed mallard glides along to and fro,
Propelled by his sturdy webbed feet paddling below.

E

is for

egret

This tall beauty with the dazzling white plumage
Maintains a regal stance at the water's edge.

elephant seal

What a show off the elephant seal with the huge bulging nose;
Grumbling and snorting, he rears up striking quite a pose.

elk

Though not natives, these majestic beasts freely roam,
Now calling the California Central Coast home.

F

is for

foal

The young horse with the wobbly legs and knobby knees
Will finish nursing, then lie down to catch a few zzzz's.

fox

This gray fellow with a long bushy tail and pointed snout
Can climb trees with his strong hooked claws to nap or hide out

frog

For such a tiny little bloke,

This guy lets out a super loud croak.

G

is for

goose

Some Canada geese like this chap can be found
On lawns and grassy fields near the coast all year round.

gopher

This pesky rodent stuffs his pocket cheeks so round,
Then pops back to the safety of his tunnel underground.

greater yellowlegs

This wary yellow-legged bird sounds an alarm
When the sudden appearance of a hawk portends harm.

H

is for

harbor seal

These true seals with spotted coats and just a hole for ears
Belly flop on rocks offshore to nap with their peers.

hawk

He stands guard on his perch with his keen eyesight;
Then spying his meal, takes off at the speed of light.

heron

While stalking, the blue long-necked bird stands ever so still,
Then with lightning speed spears his catch with his long sharp bill.

hummingbird

This iridescent green charmer has a dark head
That in the bright sunshine appears deep rosy red.

I

is for

insect

Though the kinds of insects found near the coast are many,
All have three-part bodies, six legs and two antennae.

J

is for

jay

This noisy blue-feathered chap with a black-crested head
Will boldly swoop down on your plate to pinch a piece of bread.

K

is for

killdeer

A black double-banded necklace distinguishes this shorebird,
Whose distinctive "kill-dee" call in the sandbar can be heard.

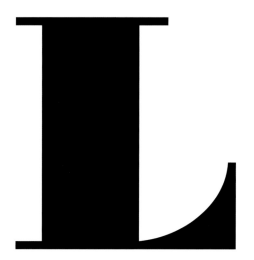

is for

lamb

The little black lamb standing next to its mama, the ewe,
Will have a white fleece just like her when it's grown up too.

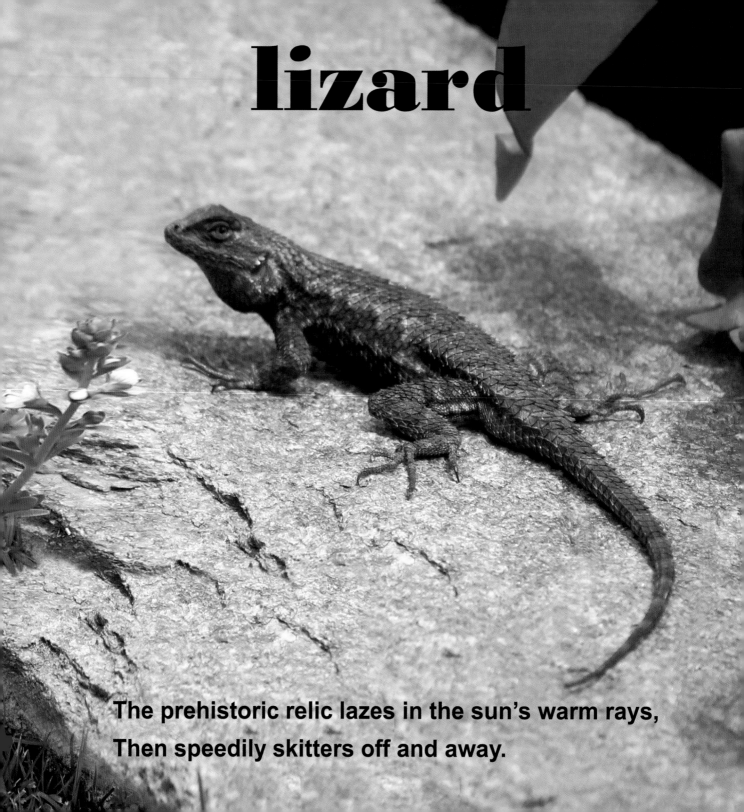

lizard

The prehistoric relic lazes in the sun's warm rays,
Then speedily skitters off and away.

longhorn

Silhouetted against miles of Central Coast foggy haze,
This long-horned fellow is king of all he surveys.

M

is for

magpie

The highly social yellow-billed magpie is found
Only in California, where it lives year round.

November brings migrating monarch butterflies in droves
To overwinter in coastal eucalyptus groves.

mountain lion

This solitary cat seldom seen in the light of day
Prowls from dusk to dawn in search of deer and other prey.

mule

Many a pack mule like this long-eared chap eating hay
Hauled supplies during construction of the Coast Highway.

N

is for

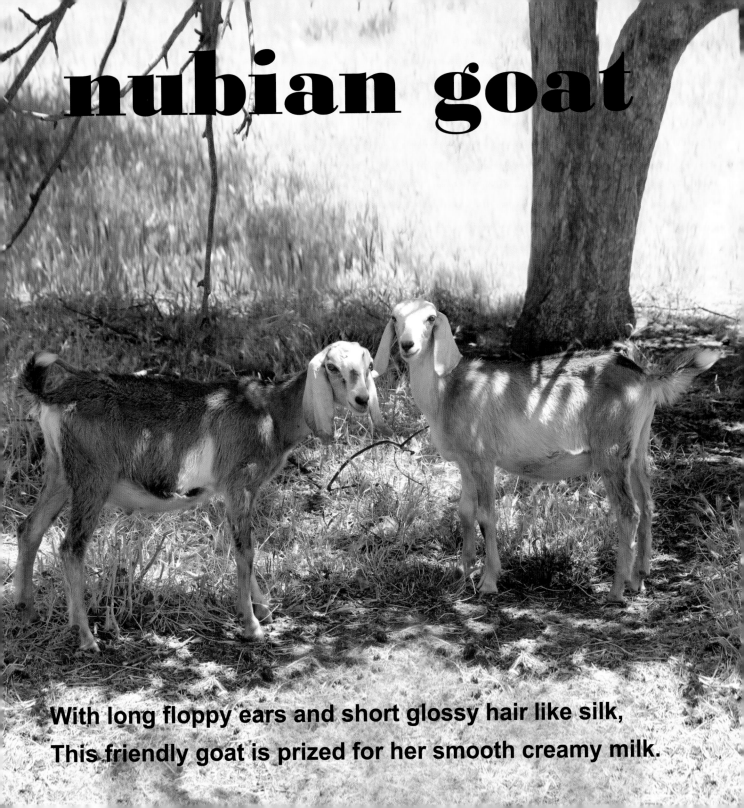

nubian goat

With long floppy ears and short glossy hair like silk,
This friendly goat is prized for her smooth creamy milk.

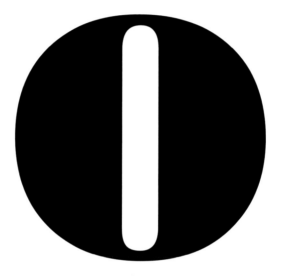

is for

opossum

This nocturnal creature with the mousy gray fur
Is known for playing dead in the face of danger.

otter

In the kelp forest, floating on his back,
He smashes shellfish for an afternoon snack.

owl

The wide-eyed "whoo"-ter hunts in the dark of night,
Then heads off to bed at morning's first light.

oystercatcher

This large black shorebird on the rocky coast eats its fill,
Prying mollusks off coastal rocks with its flat orange bill.

P

is for

pelican

This large coastal water bird is rather unique
As it scoops up fish in the pouch below its long beak.

pig

The wild sow and her piglets root through the earth,
Gobbling up yummy morsels that expand their girth.

pony

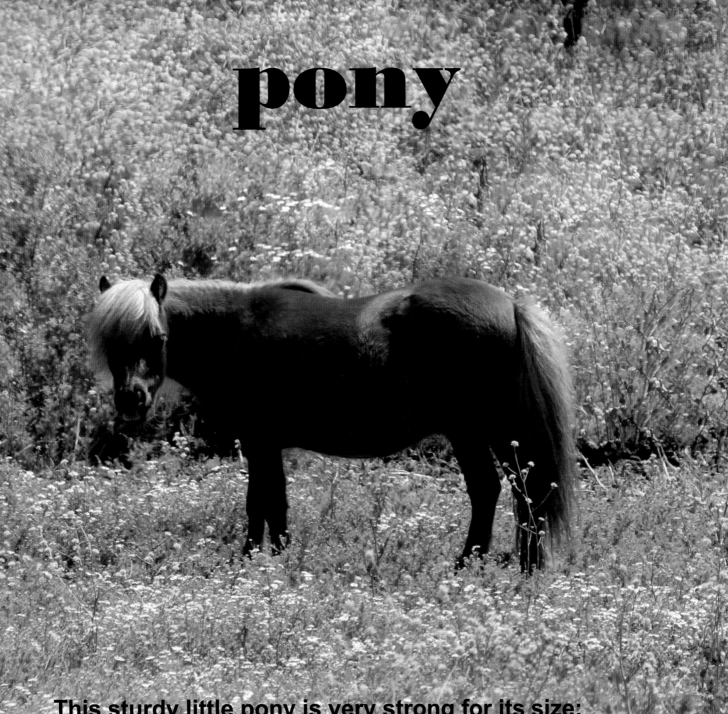

This sturdy little pony is very strong for its size;
At a birthday party one would be a welcome surprise.

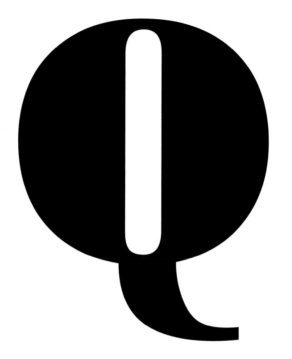

is for

quail

This plump lookout with a teardrop plume on his head
Gathered up his covey mates and away they sped.

R

is for

rabbit

This bunny with the cotton ball tail and dark tipped ears
Scampers away when a would-be predator appears.

raccoon

This "ringtail" with a black mask is familiar everywhere,
Foraging with human hand-like paws for tasty fare.

robin

The red-breasted robin that lives on the coast year round
Tilts his head while searching for tasty grubs on the ground.

is for

sea gull

This seabird is a common sight on the coastal shore;
Usually where you see one, you'll see many more.

sea lion

These playful performers sit up on their large flippers,
Barking noisily to the delight of onlookers.

sea star

If this star-shaped creature in the intertidal zone
Loses one of its arms, a new arm can be grown.

skunk

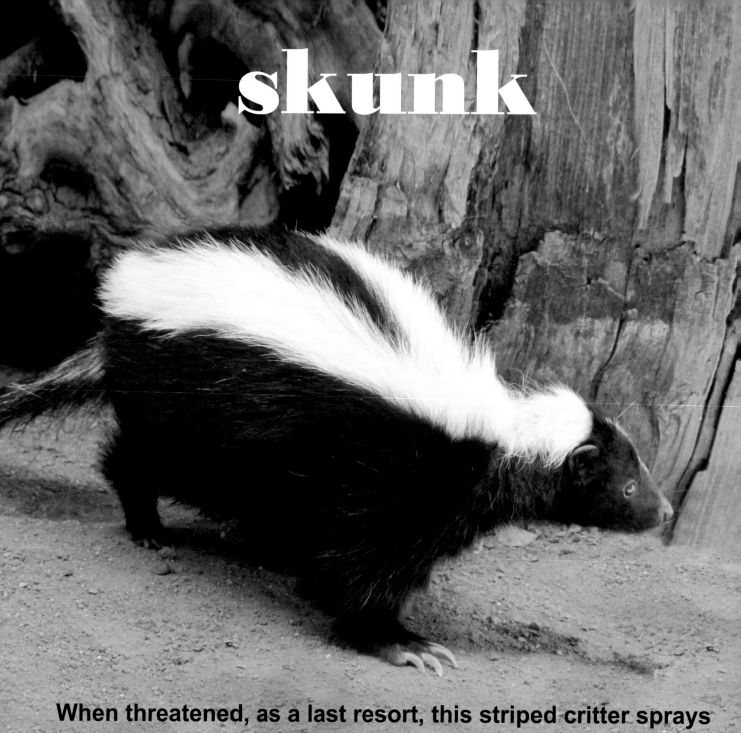

When threatened, as a last resort, this striped critter sprays
Oil with a strong foul odor that can last for days.

snail

While gardeners view snails as pests eating the plants they grow,
On French menus, they're a delicacy called *escargots*.

snake

The gopher snake slithers through the grass with great speed,
Enabling it to capture rodents on which it will feed.

squirrel

This daring acrobat with the bushy tail
Leaps from branch to branch chattering all the while.

T

is for

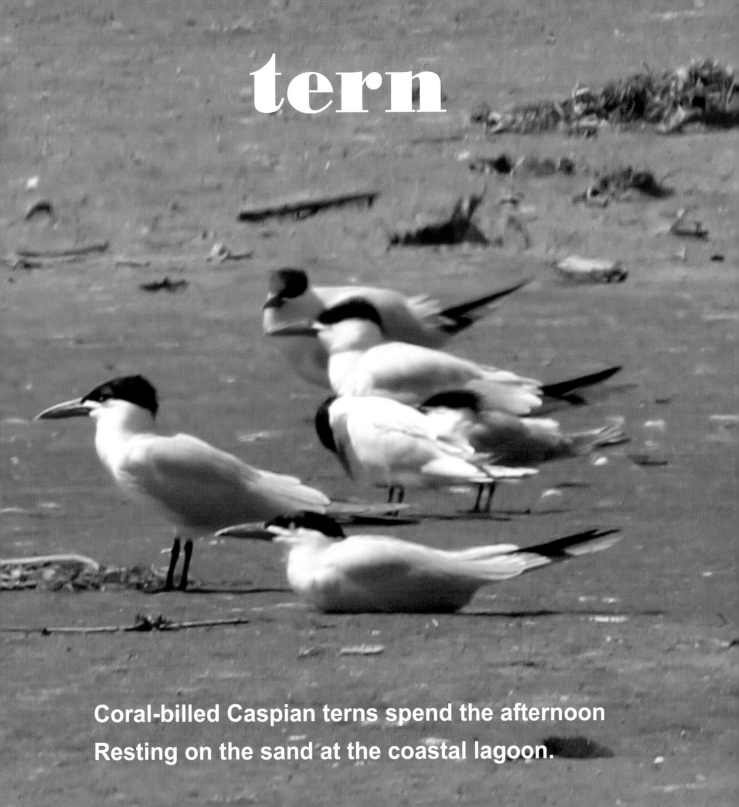

tern

Coral-billed Caspian terns spend the afternoon
Resting on the sand at the coastal lagoon.

towhee

This year-round coastal resident is most often found
Noisily scratching for bugs in dry leaves on the ground.

turkey

These plump fellows make a gobble-gobble sound,
Hunting for insects and seeds while strutting around.

U

is for

urchin

This spiny creature with a body that's round
In California coastal tide pools can be found.

V

is for

vulture

This scavenger with the naked red head hunts along auto lanes,
Foraging for carrion to feed off their lifeless remains.

W

is for

whale

Spotting a migrating giant breaching offshore,
Ecstatic whale watchers let out an earsplitting roar.

whimbrel

This shorebird with a long down-curved bill and dark striped crown
Probes the sand for small crabs and insects it then gulps down.

willet

The straight-billed willet winters on the California coastline,
Foraging for aquatic insects on which it will dine.

X

is for

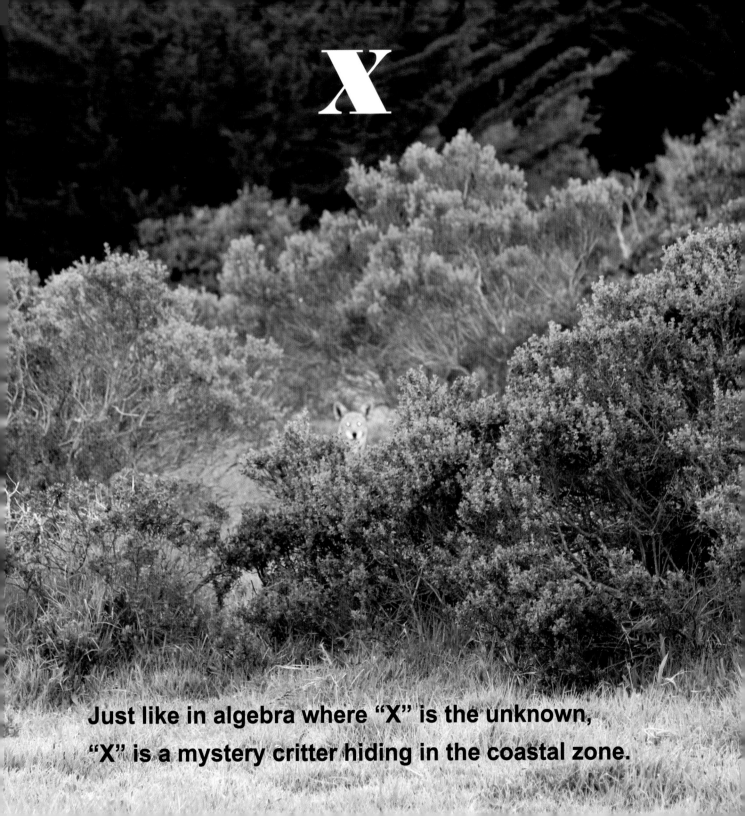

X

Just like in algebra where "X" is the unknown,
"X" is a mystery critter hiding in the coastal zone.

Y

is for

yearling colts

These young horses are free now to cavort and play;
Little do they know they'll be working one day.

Z

is for

zebra

Descended from escapees from a private zoo,
This African native is now a coastal critter too.

Website Links for Further Information

The following websites provide information about California wildlife and their habitats, viewing sites along the coast such as state parks or national reserves, and non-profit organizations that support wildlife conservation:

http://www.allaboutbirds.org/page.aspx?pid=1001 The Cornell Lab of Ornithology website page with information on birding on the California Central Coast.

http://www.bigsurcalifornia.org Big Sur Chamber of Commerce website with resource guide to Big Sur and links to sites about native wildlife.

http://www.birdwatchersdigest.com/bwdsite/learn/identification/index.php Bird Watcher's Digest website with extensive bird identification guide.

http://www.cabrillomarineaquarium.org Cabrillo Marine Aquarium website with information on aquarium exhibits, research, events and links to dozens of additional resources.

http://www.ca-ccbt.info/index.htm Central Coast Birding Trail website sponsored by Audubon-California providing a complete guide to birds in Monterey, San Luis Obispo, Santa Barbara and Ventura County birds.

http://www.cawatchablewildlife.org California Watchable Wildlife network of wildlife viewing sites throughout California searchable by region or by species.

http://www.elephantseal.org Friends of the Elephant Seal website with information on elephant seals and a live web cam view of the elephant seals at the Piedras Blancas rookery 12 miles north of Cambria and 4 miles north of Hearst Castle on Highway One. Website translated into 50 languages.

http://www.friendsofcondors.org Friends of California Condors Wild and Free website.

http://www.marinemammalcenter.org/what-we-do/rescue/our-rescue-stranding-network.html This page lists marine mammal rescue organizations in California with links to the various organizations' websites.

http://www.monarchbutterfly.org Pismo Beach Monarch Butterfly Grove website.

http://www.monarchwatch.org/download/pdf/where.pdf Monarch Program website on when and where to view monarch butterfly overwintering sites accessible to the general public on the California coast.

http://www.montereybayaquarium.org   Monterey Bay aquarium website with information on aquarium exhibits, a marine animal guide, a live ocean web cam, and much more.

http://montereybay.noaa.gov   Monterey Bay National Marine Sanctuary website with information on sanctuary wildlife viewing areas from San Francisco south to the Piedras Blancas Lighthouse north of San Simeon, including whale, dolphin and porpoise watching information.

http://www.morrobaybirdfestival.org/pages/About-Morro-Bay.aspx   Morro Bay Bird Festival website with photos and key identifying marks of Morro Bay birds as well as further website links to additional resources.

http://morrocoastaudubon.org/links.php   Morro Coast Audubon Society website with extensive links and resources relating to birds.

http://www.mycondor.org   Website managed by the Ventana Wildlife Society with profiles on the condors released into the wild at Big Sur and information on condor viewing tours.

http://www.nps.gov/index.htm   National Park Service website with information on national parks and wildlife by state and then by specific park.

http://www.parks.ca.gov   California State Park website with information on state parks by region.

http://resources.ca.gov/hearst_docs/OtherDocuments_5A-Resources_Information_Summary.pdf   A thorough report with numerous photographs on the diverse native plants, plant habitats and animal species found on the Hearst Ranch in Central California.

http://www.seaotters.org   Friends of the Sea Otter website.

http://www.sblandtrust.org/coronado-butterfly-preserve-2   Santa Barbara Land Trust website with information on preserves in Santa Barbara County, including the Coronado Butterfly Preserve and the Goleta Butterfly Grove in Goleta.

http://www.sfbaywildlife.info/index.htm   San Francisco Bay Wildlife website with guide to viewing locations and identification of mammals, birds and other classifications.

http://www.slostateparks.com   State Parks along the Luis Obispo County Coast website with information about individual parks and plants and wildlife in county parks.

http://www.ventanaws.org   Ventana Wildlife Society website with information on the Big Sur Discovery Center, native wildlife such as the condor, bald eagle and monarch butterfly in Monterey County, and related conservation programs.

About the Authors

Shirley Price grew up on the San Francisco Peninsula. She received her B.A. from the University of California, Santa Barbara, and taught elementary math and science for several years. During this time, she and Merle wrote numerous math/science teaching aids used in schools throughout the U.S. Shirley left teaching to attend the University of Southern California Law School and practiced law for twenty plus years.

Merle Price is a California Central Coast native. He received his B.S. in biology at the University of California, Santa Barbara, and taught biology, chemistry and physics at the high school level for many years before becoming a high school principal and eventually Deputy Superintendent of the Los Angeles Unified School District. He now teaches educational leadership courses at the University of California, Los Angeles, and California State University, Northridge.

The couple's primary residence is in the Southern California coastal community of Pacific Palisades. However, they spend considerable time at the family ranch on the Central Coast.